FACT FOCUS

A look at claims made

by Trump at news conference

By

Steve Palmer

The headline

In his most memorable news gathering since VP Kamala Harris turned into the Popularity based candidate for president, previous President Donald Trump said he would discuss her on Sept. 10 and pushed for two additional discussions. The conservative official chosen one represented over 60 minutes, examining various issues confronting the nation and afterward taking inquiries from journalists. He made various bogus and deluding claims. A considerable lot of them have been made previously. Here is a glance at a portion of those cases.

CROWD SIZES

CLAIM: "The biggest crowd I've ever spoken — I've spoken to the biggest crowds. Nobody's spoken to crowds bigger than me. If you look at Martin Luther King when he did his speech, his great speech, and you look at ours, same real estate, same everything, same number of people, if not we had more. And they said he had a million people, but I had 25,000 people."

THE FACTS: Trump was comparing the crowd at his speech on January 6, 2021, in front of the White House, to the crowd at Martin Luther King Jr.'s famous "I Have a Dream" speech at the Lincoln Memorial on August 28, 1963. However, the latter is thought to have hosted significantly more people than the former.

According to the National Park Service, King gave his speech at the March on Washington for Jobs and Freedom, which was attended by approximately 250,000 people. In 2021, the Associated Press reported that at least 10,000 people attended Trump's address. Besides, Trump and Ruler didn't talk in a similar area. Lord talked from the means of the Lincoln Commemoration, which looks east toward the Washington Landmark. Trump talked at the Circle, a lush region only south of the White House.

JAN. 6

 Guarantee: "No one was killed on Jan. 6." Current realities: That is bogus. Five individuals kicked the bucket in the Jan. 6, 2021, revolt and its quick fallout.

Supportive of Trump agitators penetrated the U.S. Capitol that day, as Congress tried to confirm Democrat Joe Biden's victory in the 2020 election. Among the departed are Ashli Babbitt, a Trump ally shot and killed by police, and Brian Sicknick, a cop who kicked the bucket the day subsequent to fighting the crowd. In subsequent weeks and months, four additional officers who responded to the riot committed suicide.

During the violent riot, a police officer shot and killed 35-year-old San Diego Air Force veteran Babbitt as she climbed through a broken part of a Capitol door. Trump has frequently refered to Babbitt's demise while regretting the treatment of the people who went to a convention outside the White House that day and afterward walked to the Legislative hall, large numbers of whom battled with police.

Vote based Selection

 Guarantee: "The administration was detracted from Joe Biden, and I'm no Biden fan, yet I listen for a minute, from an established outlook, from any point of view you see, they removed the administration."

Current realities: There isn't anything in the Constitution that keeps the Progressive faction from making VP Kamala Harris its candidate. The Democratic National Committee determines this procedure.

Harris formally guaranteed the designation Monday following a five-day internet casting a ballot cycle, getting 4,563 representative votes out of 4,615 cast, or around the vast majority of taking part assigns. The only other option on the ballot, "present," was supported by 52 delegates in 18 states. The VP was the main competitor qualified to get votes after no other up-and-comer qualified by the party's cutoff time following President Joe Biden's choice to exit the race on July 21.

THE ECONOMY

Claiming that things would have been different if he had succeeded Biden in office: "You wouldn't have had inflation. Because of their bad energy issues, you wouldn't have experienced inflation. Presently they've returned to the Trump thing since they need the votes. They're boring now since they needed to return since fuel was going up to 7, 8, 9 bucks a barrel."

THE FACTS: If Trump had been reelected in 2020, there would have been at least some inflation because many of the factors that cause inflation are outside of a president's control. After cooped-up Americans increased their spending on items like exercise bikes and home office furniture in 2021, which significantly disrupted supply chains, prices increased. U.S. auto organizations, for instance, couldn't get an adequate number of semiconductors and needed to pointedly diminish creation, making new and utilized vehicle costs shoot higher. As a result of Russia's invasion of Ukraine in March 2022, Ukraine's wheat exports were disrupted, and numerous nations boycotted Russian oil and gas. Food and gas prices also skyrocketed worldwide.

According to a lot of economists, including some Democrats, Biden's $1.9 trillion financial support package, which was approved in March 2021 and gave most Americans a $1,400 stimulus check, helped fuel inflation by increasing demand. In any case, it didn't cause expansion without anyone else. Furthermore, Trump upheld $2,000 improvement checks in December 2020, as opposed to the $600 checks remembered for a bundle he endorsed into regulation in December 2020. Prices continued to rise in nations with policies that differ from Biden's, such as France, Germany, and the United Kingdom, primarily as a result of the sharp rise in energy costs brought on by Russia's invasion.

IMMIGRATION

Guarantee: "Twenty million individuals came over the boundary during the Biden-Harris organization — 20 million individuals — and it very well may be particularly higher than that. No one truly knows.

" Current realities: Trump's 20 million figure is unverified, best case scenario, and he didn't give sources. U.S. Customs and Boundary Assurance reports 7.1 million captures for unlawful intersections from Mexico from January 2021 through June 2024.

That is captures, not individuals. Under pandemic-time refuge limitations, many individuals crossed at least a time or two until they succeeded in light of the fact that there were no lawful ramifications for getting turned around to Mexico. So the quantity of individuals is lower than the quantity of captures.

In addition, CBP claims that between January 2021 and June 2024, it stopped migrants 1.1 million times at official land crossings with Mexico, mostly through an online appointment system called CBP One for asylum claims.

If they had financial sponsors and arrived at an airport, nearly 500,000 migrants from Cuba, Haiti, Nicaragua, and Venezuela were also admitted by U.S. authorities under presidential authority.

That amounts to nearly 8.7 million encounters in total. Once more, the quantity of individuals is lower because of various experiences for some. There are an obscure number of individuals who escaped catch, known as "got-aways" in Boundary Watch speech. The Boundary Watch gauges the number of however doesn't distribute that number. ___ CLAIM: "She was the border czar 100%, and all of a sudden for the last few weeks she's not the border czar anymore" is the assertion made by Vice President Kamala Harris. Current realities: Harris was designated to address "main drivers" of movement in Focal America. She was not assigned to the border, but that migration manifests itself in illegal crossings into the United States.

NEW YORK CASES

 Guarantee: "The New York cases are completely controlled out of the Division of Equity." Current realities: Trump was alluding to two arguments brought against him in New York — one common and the other crook. Neither has a say in the U.S. Branch of Equity.

Letitia James, the Attorney General of New York, filed a lawsuit to start the civil case. All things considered, Trump was requested in February to suffer a $454 million consequence for lying about his abundance for quite a long time as he constructed the land realm that vaulted him to fame and the White House. The criminal case was brought by state-level prosecutor Alvin Bragg, Manhattan District Attorney.

In May, a jury viewed Trump to be blameworthy on 34 lawful offense includes in a plan to unlawfully impact the 2016 political decision through a quiet cash installment to a pornography entertainer who said the two engaged in sexual relations.

A previous adaptation of this story stirred up "last" and "previous" in the third section. A much larger audience attended Martin Luther King Jr.'s "I Have a Dream" speech on August 28, 1963, than Donald Trump's January speech near the White House. 6, 2021.

Trump told correspondents the early termination issue has "a lot of tempered down." He asserted, "I think it's actually going to be a very small issue." "It's a very small," he said.

 An ABC News/Washington Post/Ipsos survey delivered last month viewed that as 57% of Americans expressed admittance to early termination was a profoundly significant figure their vote.

The former president stated that, with some exceptions, he supports abortion, but that he believed states should decide the issue. He was gotten some information about Florida, which will have a voting form measure trying to lay out a protected right to early termination before fetal reasonability. Trump said he would hold a question and answer session about the subject "sooner or later soon."

Florida has a vote coming up on that, and I figure most likely the vote will go in somewhat more liberal manner than individuals naturally suspected. In any case, I'll declare that at the fitting time," he said.

Trump says Harris' 'vacation' will go on through DNC

Harris and Walz are currently traveling to seven battleground states on a campaign tour.

Trump said he was not doing likewise kind of visit since he believed he was driving in those states. He additionally anticipated that Harris' "wedding trip period" won't keep going long. "Gracious, it will end. The honeymoon phase will soon come to an end. He stated, "Look, she's got a little period and a convention coming up."

Previous President Trump attempted to hold onto back the titles and control VP Harris' political decision energy Thursday with a long and typically meandering news meeting at his Blemish a-Lago domain in Florida.

Trump seems irritated by Harris' ascent in the surveys following President Biden's choice to move to one side from the 2024 race. Harris, who has also benefited from a energized Democratic base and a significant increase in fundraising, has substantially reduced Trump's lead over Biden. The news meeting was plainly an endeavor by the previous president to pull together the focus on himself after a period during which Harris has delighted in generally certain consideration and has held onto all important focal point.

TRUMP PROPOSE THREE DISCUSSION

The primary news out of the question and answer session was the previous president's idea that he and Harris ought to partake in three broadcast discusses.

Trump proposed a Sept. 4 conflict on Fox News, a Sept. 10 discussion on NBC and a Sept. 25 experience on ABC. Prior to this, debates had a murky picture. Trump had suggested he was done ready to take part in a planned ABC conflict, while the Harris lobby had shown she was probably not going to consent to his counterproposal for a discussion on Fox. Presently, maybe the ABC discussion will go for it. Early reports demonstrate NBC is in chats with the two missions, while Harris actually has not expressed yes to a Fox banter.

Any conflict between the two applicants would be a gigantic television occasion. Trump is unlikely to win a debate as decisively as he did on June 27, when Biden made catastrophic errors. However, the previous president will be anxious to demonstrate that he can go one-on-one with Harris and wring advantage from the occasion.

Harris is berated by Trump for a lack of press conferences.

 Since becoming the de facto Democratic nominee, Harris's failure to participate in a news conference or unscripted interview has been a line of attack from the Trump camp over the past few days.

That objection has been made when Harris has drawn huge and clear excitement to her assemblies — particularly since her decision of Minnesota Gov. as her running mate, Tim Walz (D). Trump attempted to prod Harris into such an appearance Thursday. At a certain point, he said "she can't do a news meeting," claiming Harris was "not brilliant enough" to do as such.

He additionally demonstrated Harris was declining to try and do interviews since, he guaranteed, "she's scarcely able." The adequacy of this hectoring appears to be available to discuss. Harris is not going to act solely on Trump's insistence that she should. Yet, the previous president's attention on her absence of unscripted appearances will reverberate in the media and may add to the tension upon her. The hope of Team Trump is that a mistake by Harris could quickly bring her campaign back to earth.

Trump looks to paint Harris and Walz as extremists

 The campaign of the former president is eager to portray Harris and her running mate as outside the mainstream of American society. Thursday, Trump extended that effort.

He fought Harris "annihilated San Francisco" during her experience as the city's lead prosecutor. He likewise thrashed the VP for her record on the line, refering to the once-inescapable portrayal of her as Biden's "line dictator." Be that as it may, Trump was likewise decided in pursuing Walz, who he said has been "weighty into the transsexual world" — and whom he by and large cast as an extreme left figure. Trump asserted that the two constitute the "radical left."

Doubtlessly this depiction of Harris and Walz will keep on being a fundamental topic of conservative assaults. Naturally, Harris and Walz are exerting significant effort to counter those jabs. Liberals trust Harris' record as an investigator and Walz's Midwestern "standard person" persona will prevail upon electors.

An impossible guard of Biden

 The news meeting incorporated a few indiscernible minutes when Trump offered a safeguard, of a sort, of Biden. At one point, Trump suggested that the method by which Harris had replaced the president as the Democratic standard-bearer might have been "unconstitutional," asserting that the "presidency was taken away from Joe Biden."

 Trump also mentioned that Biden got 14 million votes in the Democratic primary, which Harris obviously didn't challenge in any way. Even Trump acknowledged that his use of such language was odd. "I honestly hate his, as you've presumably seen," he recognized at a certain point, alluding to Biden. Trump's motivation for employing the strategy is clear.

He is trying to stir up elector disappointment about how Biden was replaced by Harris. Given the speed with which Democrats have rallied around Harris, there is little evidence that the strategy is working.

An unusual aside about Dr. Martin Luther Lord Jr.

It is common for Trump events to be diverted into unusual and sometimes harmful tangents. That happened on Thursday, when Trump responded to a question about the riot on Jan. 6 with a bizarre and snarky series of remarks about Dr. Speech by Martin Luther King Jr. titled "I Have A Dream" in 1968.

In particular, Trump fought the group that accumulated for his discourse close to the Oval on Jan. 6, 2021, which went before the uproar at the State house, drew a greater group than Lord's milestone social equality address.

In addition to the fact that the claim is false, Trump appears ill-advised to engage in such a bizarre dispute. The issue of race is as of now delicate in the current year's race — and not just on the grounds that Trump's rival is a lady of Dark and South Asian plummet.

Trump claimed Harris only adopted a Black identity when it was politically advantageous to her during a recent appearance before the National Association of Black Journalists. Those comments caused a tumult. For no apparent reason, Trump has now opened a new rift in the race-related controversy.